Take a trip to
LIBYA

Richard Tames

Franklin Watts

London   New York   Sydney   Toronto

Facts about Libya

Area:
1,759,540 sq. km.
(679,362 sq. miles)

Population:
3,955,000

Capital:
Tripoli (1,000,000)

Largest Cities:
Benghazi (500,000)
Zawia (244,000)
Misurata (194,000)
Homs (161,000)

Official language:
Arabic

Religion:
Islam

Main Exports:
Oil, gas, esparto grass

Currency:
Dinar

Franklin Watts
12a Golden Square
London W1

Franklin Watts Inc.
387 Park Avenue South
New York, N.Y. 10016

ISBN: UK Edition 0 86 313 807 1
ISBN: US Edition 0–531–10653–5
Library of Congress Catalog Card No:
88-51321
© Franklin Watts Limited 1989

Typeset by Lineage, Watford
Printed in Hong Kong

Maps: Simon Roulestone
Design: Edward Kinsey

Stamps: Stanley Gibbons Limited
Photographs: Dr J.A. Allan 5, 12, 14, 15,
16, 20, 21, 22, 24, 25, 27, 28, 31; Hutchison
Library 4, 7, 10, 11, 18, 19, 26, 30; Christine
Osborne 13, 29; ZEFA 3, 6, 17, 23

Front Cover: ZEFA
Back Cover: Hutchison Library

Libya is Africa's fourth largest country, but it is thinly populated. Part of the world's biggest desert, the Sahara, covers more than nine-tenths of Libya. The Sahara contains large areas of sand, stony plains and rocky uplands.

The capital, Tripoli, lies on the
Mediterranean Sea in northwestern
Libya. Most Libyans live on the coast in
or near Tripoli. Many others live around
Beghazi, on or near the northeastern
coast.

4

Going south from the Mediterranean coast, you leave behind well-watered farmland. Bordering the coastal plains is a dry region where esparto grass is often found. This grass is used to make fine writing paper.

The Sahara covers 9,065,000 sq km (3,500,000 sq miles). It contains vast depressions in which there are oases, such as Kufra, Sabhah and Ghadames. Oases are places in deserts where there is water. Traders used to cross the desert by going from one oasis to the next.

Libya has a hot, dry climate. The world's highest temperature, measured in the shade, 58°C (136.4°F), was recorded at Al Aziziyah. The average rainfall in the Sahara is less than 12.5cm (5 inches) a year. Libya has no permanent rivers. When rare storms occur, streams flow along the valleys for a short time.

The picture shows some of the money and stamps used in Libya. The main unit of currency is the dinar, which is divided into 1,000 millemes.

WORLD MAP

LIBYA

ITALY

GREECE

Mediterranean Sea

TUNISIA

Tripoli

Homs

Al Bayda

Derna
Tobruk

Misratah

Benghazi

Al
Aziziyah

Surt

Gulf of Sirte

Ghadames

ALGERIA

LIBYA

Sabhah

EGYPT

Sahara

Kufra

▲ Bette Peak

NIGER

SUDAN

CHAD

9

Tripoli has been the capital of Libya since the country became independent in 1951. The city and its suburbs contain about a third of Libya's total population. Tripoli is also the country's main port.

Most Libyans are Arabs, though there are some Berbers in the west. The Berbers, who also include some nomadic Tuaregs in the desert, lived in North Africa before the Arabs. About a fifth of workers in Libya are from other countries. The picture shows people at the oasis settlement of Ghadames.

About 50,000 years ago, during the Ice Age, the Sahara was covered by massive shallow lakes and lush vegetation. Cave paintings prove that people lived there. By Roman times, the climate had changed and the vegetation had gone. So had the people.

Libya was once part of the empire of the Phoenicians, a trading people who came from what is now Lebanon. They founded the city of Leptis Magna in about 600 BC. The Romans took it over in 46 BC. The ruins near Homs are among the most impressive of all Roman Africa.

The Ancient Greeks founded the city of Cyrene in northeast Libya in about 630 BC. It grew rich on trading in medicines and its people were famous as doctors. In 96 BC the Romans took it over and made it a provincial capital.

The Arabs conquered Libya in
AD 643. The Berbers soon adopted the
Arab religion, Islam. This mosque is in
southern Libya. The tower is used by an
official called a muezzin, who calls people
when it is time for them to say their
prayers.

The Arabs brought the Arabic
language with them and today it is
Libya's official language. The Berber
language also survives. This picture
shows notices in Arabic on new blocks of
housing. Some educated people also
speak Italian and English.

16

Islam greatly influences the Libyan way of life. The country's laws and the things children learn at school are based on Islam. This is the mosque of Sidi Beliman in Tripoli. Libya gives money to poor countries where Islam is the main religion.

Until 1969, Libya was a kingdom. Now it calls itself a "Jamahiriya" — an Arabic word which means "a state of the masses". Since 1977, ordinary people have been encouraged to take part in government at every level.

Colonel Muammar al-Gaddafi has
been Libya's leader since 1969. Many
Libyans admire him for using the wealth
from the oil industry to improve the
country. But many Western leaders do
not trust him and say that he has helped
terrorists in many parts of the world.

Libya was a poor country until oil was discovered in 1958. Libya is Africa's second largest oil producer after Nigeria. Money from oil sales has been used to improve the people's diet, health and education. Libya also produces natural gas.

Oil is used as the raw material in the fast-growing, chemical industry. Libya has some iron ore, salt, gypsum and sulphur. There is an iron and steel plant at Misratah, Libya's fourth largest city. Cement making is the other major industry.

Only about eight per cent of Libya can
be farmed or used for grazing, but about
a fifth of the workforce is employed in
farming. Olive groves, like the one
shown here, are found near the coast.
Wheat and barley are the main grain
crops.

Dates are grown at desert oases, together with such crops as maize (corn). The government is paying for large irrigation projects to increase the area of farmland. At present, Libya imports four-fifths of what it needs to feed its growing population.

Water is needed for livestock. In the desert, herdsmen come to oases to water their animals. Libya has more than 6,000,000 sheep and 1,500,000 goats. Pigs are not kept because Muslims are forbidden by their religion to eat pork.

Libyan craftsmen show great skill in working with such materials as wood and leather, textiles and metals. This fine piece of silver is often worn by women to show their family's wealth.

Education is free in Libya and about half of all adults can read and write. Libya has too few educated people, which explains why many foreigners work there. The children in the picture are not at school. They are dressed up for a special occasion.

In 1960, less than a quarter of the population lived in towns and cities. By 1985, three out of every five did. People, like this Tuareg, who live in a village far from any city, follow a way of life which is fast disappearing.

Shopping in Libya is controlled by the
government, which decides on prices and
what sort of goods will be imported. Big
supermarkets, like the one in the picture,
are replacing small private shops.

The diet of most Libyans has improved greatly in recent years. "Kebabs" — pieces of meat and vegetables, roasted on a skewer — are popular, as also is mint tea. Many people enjoy Western-style soft drinks, but Islam forbids beer or wine to be drunk.

The government has built many new homes in recent years. This poster contrasts high-rise buildings with city slums. Many Libyan nomads have been reluctant to give up their tents. Even Colonel Gadaffi is known to prefer a tent to a Western-style home.

In 1983, Libya decided to build a
"Great Man-made River" to pump up
water from under the Sahara and pipe it
to the farms along the coast. In this way,
Libya will be able to grow more of its own
food in the 1990s. This picture shows the
laying of the pipeline.

Index